FUNNY JOKES

14 YEAR OLD

DARE YOU NOT TO LAUGH CHALLENGE

Totally Awesome Joke Book for Teens

HERE AT LAST!
We have taken the Try Not to Laugh
Challenge to the Next Level!

LOL　　　　　　　　　*LOL*

Introducing
The Dare You Not to Laugh Challenge™
for Teens!
If surviving the teen years isn't
challenging enough, here comes the
best teen cringe-worthy collection
of jokes that are teen-themed
and designed to squeak out a laugh
or two! Don't miss out on all
the fun and eye rolls!

We Dare You Not to Laugh
or at least Smile!

LOL　　　　*LOL*

Everyone knows that Albert Einstein was a genius...
but his brother Frank was a real monster!

What do you call a mummy
with a cold?

Sir Cough, I guess.

This is Bob.
Bob has no arms.

"Knock, knock."
"Who is it?"
"It isn't Bob."

An apple additiction is the worst.

You can't see a doctor about it.

My teacher thinks that I am
obsessed with astronomy.

What planet does he live on?

My mom uses outdated technology.

I have the FAX to prove it.

Snow White took six dwarfs to the
dentist.

None of them were HAPPY.

What was Shakespeare known for?

He put the Lit in Literature!

Why can't PC gamers use Uber?

Too many incompatible drivers.

What is the opposite of Silly String?

Serious String.

What kind of bread do teens make sandwiches with?

Whole YEET bread.

bruh

[bur-uh] noun.

The ultimate response to anything, any situation, or anyone: meaning varies with tone, volume and emphasis.

Guess who I bumped into on my way to pick up my replacement contacts?

Everybody!

If video games resembled a human body, what would be the worst part?

Defeat!

On weekdays I wake up grumpy.

On the weekends I let my little brother sleep in.

What do cowboy ghosts wear?

BOOO-TS!

What are the nicest colors?

Complimentary colors.

Want to hear a good joke about procrastinators.....

You really should try playing paintball blindfolded.

You don't know what you're missing!

Why did the IT guy go to the hospital?

He touched the firewall!

I ordered a reversible jacket.

I can't wait to see how it TURNS OUT.

Chances are if you've seen one shopping center, you've seen a mall.

I couldn't get tickets to Elton John's Farewell Tour so...
I think it's gonna be a long, long time before I see him in concert.

Well, that's not right.

What kind of doctor was Dr. Pepper?

A FIZZ-ician.

Who is the fastest clothing designer in the world?

Taylor SWIFT!

There are so many new haircuts
to try this year.

I will need to MULLET them over before
I decide.

I asked my mom if she could make
my favorite Asian dish.

Sushi did.

Why didn't Dracula get into art
school?

He could only draw blood.

What happens if you and a mummy
fart at the same time?

Toot in common.

I just watched a video on how
to do a silly dance jig.

It's a step-by-step guide.

I was attacked by 9, 11, 13, and 15.

The odds were against me.

What did the quarterback say
to the football?

Catch you later.

Don't swallow a book on synonyms.

You will have the thesaurus throat
ever.

What do you call a pile of cats?

A PURR-amid.

A weasel walks into a restaurant. The waiter says, "This is a first, I've never served a weasel before! What can I get you?"

"Pop," goes the weasel.

teenager

[teen-ey-jer] noun.

A person who is better prepared for a zombie apocalypse than for school tomorrow.

Don't let your dog eat any
Scrabble tiles.

It could spell disaster.

Beware of angry hamburgers.
One just flipped on me.

What do you call a tiny mother?

A Minimom!

How does a panda make flapjacks?

With a pan-DUH!

What kind of lights did Noah use
on the Ark?

FLOODlights.

What do you call a baby potato?

A tater tot.

What do you call a singing computer?

A DELL.

Why are swimmers good at soccer?

Because they dive a lot.

If you haven't tried boba tea,
you should give it a pearl.

Where can you always find money?

In the dictionary.

What did the drummer name his
triplets?

Anna One, Anna Two, Anna Three.

I broke up with my old console.

Nothing was wrong with my Xbox,
but it was time for a Switch.

I PAUSED MY
GAME
TO BE HERE

Dolphin puns are terrible.

On porpoise.

Where do you learn to make ice cream?

Sundae school.

What is the opposite of a croissant?

A happy uncle.

What did the clock ask the watch?

HOUR are you doing?

What do you call two witches who
who live together?

Broommates.

How do trees get on the internet?

They log in!

You have to wonder why some people always have graph paper with them.

They must be plotting something...

cell phone

[sel fohn] noun.

The easiest way to look cool when you are in public by yourself.

Why is Ed Sheeran's favorite cereal rainbow Lucky Charms?

He's in love with the shape of U!

What is harder to catch the faster you run?

Your breath.

Which Jedi won the lottery?

Obi-WON.

Why did the kid eat his dollar bill?

Because it was his lunch money!

Why do shoemakers go to heaven?

They have good soles.

It's all fun and games until someone loses a weiner.

Who is the corniest dad?

Jiffy Pop.

What has five fingers, but isn't your hand?

My hand!

Where does a baseball player go when he needs a new uniform?

New Jersey.

Why can you always tell what Dick and Jane will do next?

Because they are so easy to read.

Who keeps the tooth fairy busy?

Hockey players.

Who is the best-dressed singer
in the world?

Harry STYLES.

Do you want to hear a joke about dogs?

It is a little far-fetched.

Don't bother going to an
Air and Space Museum.

There is NOTHING there.

textciting

[tekst-sahy-ting] noun.

The group chat you text in when
something really good happens
to you.

Sometimes spilling the tea can take
Oolong time.

To the man who invented zero:

Thanks for NOTHING.

Why didn't Cinderella make the basketball team?

She had a pumpkin for a coach.

What is a duck's favorite sea monster?

A Quacken.

What do witches do when it rains?

They get wet.

Why do giraffes make bad pets?

They are too HIGH maintenance.

In what sport do winners move
backward and losers move ahead?

Tug of War.

What is a snake's favorite subject?

Hiss-tory!

What does a computer do when it
is tired?

It crashes.

TEE HEE

How do you feel after winning
a hotdog eating contest?

Aw-FULL!

I would be happy to give away
my broken guitar for free.

No strings attached.

YUK-YUK

A movie theater was robbed of over
$500 dollars.

The thieves took a jumbo bag of popcorn,
two large sodas, and a box of
Raisonets.

MATH

The only place where people buy
77 watermelons and
no one wonders
WHY....

Don't limp in here late with a lame excuse!

Why is AC/DC always hungry for something sweet in the morning?

Because it's a long way to the bakeshop if you want a danish roll.

What do you call a horse that roams?

Unstable.

What always gets overlooked in
the backyard?

The garden fence.

Why does Superman throw so many
dinner parties?

Because he's a SUPPER-hero!

Parents should teach their kids
sign language.

It might come in handy.

Peter Pan jokes...

they never get old.

What do students taking finals and mufflers have in common?

Both are always EXHAUSTED.

Which football player wears the biggest helmet?

The one with the biggest head.

What's an egg's least favorite meal?

BREAK-fast!

Did you know that librarians are fast runners?

They know how to BOOK it.

What is the smartest cell in the body?

The STEM cell.

Students should have special powers to help them get through 12 years of school.

But all they get is SUPERVISION.

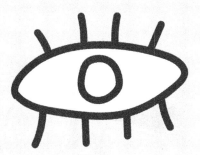

Where do bad rainbows go?

Prism.

Stairs can't be trusted.

They are always up to something.

What do pigs and ink have in common?

They both belong in a pen.

Did you hear the one about the giant throwing up?

It's all over town.

Don't get mad at lazy people.

They didn't do anything.

Where did the hacker go?

He ransomware.

How do you weigh a millennial?

In Instagrams.

What color is the wind?

Blew.

What is the term for owning too many dogs?

A ROVER-load.

Don't spell part backwards,
it is a trap!

I bought a giant elephant for
my bedroom...

but I don't want to talk about it.

Rap is like scissors.

It always loses to ROCK.

How does Zeus make the best
fries ever?

Ancient Greece.

What word starts with E and ends with E but only has one letter in it?

Envelope.

Migraines aren't real.

They're all in your head.

Where do boats go when they get sick?

The dock.

I didn't like skydiving school.

So I dropped out!

Why was Bigfoot looking for two giant bananas?

He wanted a pair of slippers!

Hide & Seek Champion

How does Bigfoot tell time?

With a SASQ-watch!

Student: " Why is that book
so thick?"

Teacher: "It's a long story."

What kind of prize do you get
if you don't exercise for a year?

A Trophy!

Did you hear about the dog who
evaporated?

He will be mist!

Picking your nose in an elevator
is wrong.

On so many levels.

Do they allow LOUD laughing in Hawaii?

Or just a low ha?

Science Teacher: "What are clouds made of?"

Student: "A collection of massive computer servers."

What do you do if a sink is pounding on your door?

You let that sink in.

Stevie Nicks is releasing a new album.

I usually don't follow music trends, but I've heard Rumours.

A friend gave me some Play-Doh.

Not sure what to make of it.

Student: "What music did you listen to when you were younger?"

Teacher: "Led Zepplin."

Student: "Who?"

Teacher: "Yup, I listened to them too."

Why doesn't a proton need a suitcase?

Because it's traveling light.

Can you believe that there are tickets on sale for a concert that only costs 45 cents?

50 Cent is the warm-up band for Nickelback.

maybe

[mey-bee] noun.

I secretly mean absolutely NO.

How do you make a sloth fast?

Take away its food.

What do you call a zombie who likes to stir-fry his food?

Dead man WOK-ing.

I wanted to wear my camo hat.

But I couldn't find it.

My sister accidentally ordered limited-seating tickets for the Elton John concert.

My sister is happily seated, but I'm still standing.

What did the Lego alien say?

"I come in PIECES."

My friend does not know what oblivious means.

He really has no idea.

What kind of car does an egg drive?

A YOLKSwagen.

How do crabs get to school?

They use the SIDE WALK.

Did you know that there is a street in England that is named after Harry Styles?

It only goes in ONE DIRECTION, though.

Why can't blind people eat ocean fish?

Because it's SEE food!

Don't insult a banana.

You'll hurt its PEELINGS.

Don't donate to causes that sponsor marathons.

They just take the money and RUN.

Where is the best place to do math homework in New York City?

Times Square.

Why did the soda bottle take music lessons?

It wanted to be a POP star.

How do you respect BTS?

You Bow Wow Wow.

What is Jin's favorite song?

Jin-gle Bells.

Where do lions, elephants, hippos, and cheetahs fly?

On the African PLAIN.

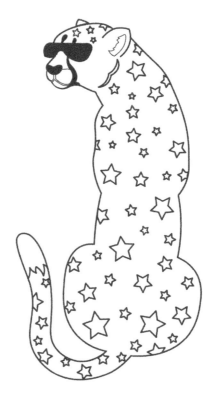

Did you hear about the guy who invented the knock-knock joke?

He got the "No-Bell" prize.

My teacher told me to have a good day. So I went home.

What can you say about NASCAR champions?

They have DRIVE.

Last night I had a dream that I weighed less than a thousandth of a gram.

I was like, 0 mg.

There is a new rap song about shampoo.

It's fine. The lyrics are CLEAN.

I before e

except when eighty hippieish foreign concertmeisters are boogieing by tippytoeing kaleidoscopic rottweilers & yuppieish snowshoeing weisenheimer heifers.

WEIRD.

My wallet is like an onion.

When I open it, it makes me cry.

Teacher: "Why are you talking to yourself?"

Student: "I needed some expert advice."

What do you call an old man who is good at playing soccer?

Gerry Hat-trick.

I cracked a joke last night.
Now I can't use it again.

Why were the burger and fries
running?

Because they are fast food.

How did Freddy Mercury die?

He bit the dust.

Don't make jokes about Eminem
and M&M's candy.

He's just a wrapper.

The King of the Jungle said he
was a tiger.

He was LION.

Why do dads tell bad jokes
to their kids?

They just want to help them
become GROAN-ups.

YUK-YUK

PULL YOURSELF TOGETHER MAN!

Kid: "Dad, I'm hungry, will the pizza bagels be long?"

Dad: "No, they will probably be round."

I wasn't going to have a brain transplant, but then I changed my mind.

Bread is just like the sun's orbital path.

It rises in the YEAST and sets in the WAIST.

A storm blew 25% of my roof off last night.

OOF.

Why don't people gossip during breakfast?

They don't want to spill the tea.

Why was the mechanic's fashion show boring?

There wasn't enough time to change attire.

What is the worst thing about being a birthday cupcake?

After you are set on fire, you are eaten by the hero who saved you!

What does Alexa eat for breakfast?

Siri-al.

Wood-Fired Pizza.

Where will pizza get a job now?

What Beatles song hit the top of the charts in Italy?

PENNE Lane.

Why are tacos like the
speed of light?

Because they sure go fast.

What do you call an FBI
barbecue party?

A steak out.

Where does a myth buster sleep?

In debunk bed.

Mariah Carey just bought a large farm that has every farm animal on it except for sheep.

All she wants for Christmas is EWE.

What happens if you cross the nursery rhyme, "This little piggy went to market" with rock and roll music?

A TOE JAM.

If money doesn't grow on trees then...

why do banks have branches?

Student: "I fell and scraped my knee in two places."

School Nurse: "Then don't go to those two places."

What happens to a square when it has an accident?

It turns into a WRECK-tangle.

What is a dung beetle's favorite candy?

Feces Pieces

What is something you let go, but no one will try to catch it?

A fart.

Don't bother telling a bald man a hair-raising story.

How much does a rainbow weigh?

Not much, it is pretty light.

I recently learned sign language.

So I can tell jokes that people haven't HEARD before.

What can you do for a sad astronaut?

Give him some spaceman.

Why can't you trust a mattress?

It is always lying behind your back.

How do bees get to school?

They take the buzzzzz.

I was looking for a password that was eight characters long.

So I picked Snow White and the seven dwarfs.

How are hockey players like aquarium fish?

You tap on the glass to get their attention.

What do you call the Terminator when he retires?

The EXterminator.

What do you call a zombie who doesn't joke around?

Dead serious.

What do you say about people who star gaze?

Things are looking up!

What kind of insect farts a lot?

STINK bugs.

Roses are red
I could scream
Shawn Mendes falls onstage
& instantly becomes a meme

What is the highest rank in the
popcorn army?

Colonel.

Well, that's not
a good sign.

Don't interrupt people when they
are working on a puzzle.

You might hear some CROSSWORDS.

How do you greet a succulent?

Aloe.

I'm Sorry.
Did I just
Roll my Eyes
Out Loud?

What do you call an insect
with a perm?

FRISbee.

It's fun to tell jokes about the Rolling Stones.

In fact, it's a gas, gas, gas.

Do you know what's so great about being a skull?

You don't need NOBODY.

Where do cats keep their lipstick?

In their PURRRS.

Why don't basketball players go on vacation?

They are not allowed to TRAVEL.

You should try paintball someday.

It's worth a SHOT!

Why wasn't the kid excited about playing soccer?

He was just doing it for the KICKS.

What do you call a noble cow?

Sir Loin.

What is a sweet way to get rich?

Eat FORTUNE cookies.

What do ghosts drink in the summertime?

GHOULaid.

Voldemort, "So...I just have to lie?"

Pinocchio, "Yep."

Have you ever let out a huge sigh of relief when you pass a test that you thought you bombed?

Only a PHEW will understand.

What did the aggravated chef grill for dinner?

SHEESH kebabs.

Funny how the show Spongebob Squarepants was named after him.

We all know that Patrick was the STAR.

Where is Frankenstein from?

All Over!

Why are skeletons so calm?

Nothing gets under their skin.

What do you call leftover lettuce?

The romaines.

Infinity, everlasting, timeless, eternal...
The list is endless.

Why can't you walk away
from an Italian dessert?

You cannoli run.

Do you know that Ed Sheeran's
daughter is missing?

Sheeran away.

Why can't astronauts eat popsicles?

In space, no one can hear the
ice cream truck.

It would be cool if an archeologist found a fossilized dragon fart.

That would be a blast from the past.

What do you call a guy in debt?

Owen.

What do you call a guy with a rubber toe?

Roberto!

How do you search for fart jokes?

POO-gle.

What do you call a cow fart?

Dairy air.

What farm animal is famous?

G.O.A.T.!

Why are farts unsuccessful in social media?

Nobody wants to follow them!

I have decided that RACKETball isn't for me.

Way too NOISEY.

Everyone should get a universal remote.

It CHANGES everything!

JUST BECAUSE
**I'M AWAKE
DOESN'T MEAN**
I'M READY TO DO THINGS

Time flies like an arrow, but fruit flies like a banana.

What do runners eat before a race?

Nothing, they fast!

How do you get a couple of avocados
into an Aerosmith concert?

Tell them to "GUAC This Way!"

Where do ghosts post their videos?

BOOtube.

I really don't care if I don't know
how to spell armageddon.

It's not the end of the world.

How do you make the number one disappear?

You add a G and it's GONE.

hold your horses
[hohld yoo hawrses] phrase.

Imaginary horses that keep you from doing something too soon.

What do planets like to read?

Comet books.

What do you call a person with seven fingers?

Three fingers short.

What did the Earth say to the
other planets?

Get a life!

My kids said that they will scream
if I put another Britney Spears song
in my playlist.

But oops, I did again.

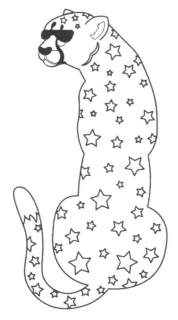

Where do geologists go out to eat?

Hard Rock Cafe.

What do you call a person with no body and no nose?

Nobody knows.

I've got your back!

I was looking for a good U2 joke, but I couldn't find what I was looking for.

Where do mermaids look for jobs?

The KELP-wanted section.

What do you call a mathematician who spent all summer in the sun?

A TANGENT.

As hard as I try, I haven't been able to finish learning the whole alphabet.

I don't know Y.

What do you get when you cross
a tiger with a zebra?

A tiger.

How did the author run so fast?

He knew how to BOOK it!

I am leaving now

[i am lee-ving nou] phrase.

Not really, I still have to get
dressed and find my shoes.

The gravity joke is getting a little old, but people FALL for it all the time.

Don't stare at a glass of lemonade.

Take a PITCHER, it will last longer.

Shout out to my grandma!

That's the only way she can hear.

How funny are mountains?

They're HILL AREAS!

Why are robots so brave?

Because they have nerves of steel.

How do you feed the entire school with one loaf of bread?

You cut the ends off and now you have endless bread!

Why was the chef arrested?

He was beating the eggs.

ha-ha
[hah-hah] phrase.

I really don't think it's funny,
but I want to stay on your good side.

Why are ghosts bad liars?

Because you can see right through
them.

How much does it cost Santa to fly around the world on Christmas Eve?

Eight BUCKS.

Someone stole my mood ring.

Not sure how I feel about that.

What is number two's special day?

Tuesday.

My friend invented an invisible drone.

I can't see it taking off.

What kind of keys are sweet?

Cookies.

My brother always knows what is in a wrapped present.

It's a GIFT.

When do you bring your dad to school?

When you have a POP quiz.

What did the ice cube say to the water?

I was water before I got COOL.

What kind of ant fights crime?

A vigilANTe.

TACO CAT
SPELLED BACKWARDS IS

TACO CAT

Why was the doorknob mad?

It didn't get its turn.

Why did the cornstalk start crying?

Because the farmer ripped his
ears off!

Why shouldn't you eat comic books?

Because they would taste funny!

My favorite coffee mug is one
year old.

FRAPPE Birthday to You!

How do monsters like their eggs?

Terri-FRIED!

The guy wondered why the frisbee was getting bigger.

Then it HIT him.

Who tells the funniest jokes in a candy factory?

The LOL-ipop!

How does a gamer make bread?

With Ninten-DOUGH!

Where do crayons go on vacation?

COLOR-ado.

What do people and video games have in common?

Everyone always argues over which generation was the best.

How do you throw an outer space party?

You PLANET.

What type of cheese is made backwards?

Edam.

What is a robot's favorite snack?

Computer chips.

I can't believe that viruses can just get into my body without my permission!

It makes me sick.

I'm going to bed
[ahy-em goh-ing tuh bed] phrase.

I'm really tired of texting with you.

Today my friend ate 3 large pizzas.

That's ODD.

Why are we trying to make burgers out of plants?

Haven't cows been doing that for like, forever?

Why are open doors good for storing things?

Because they are AJAR.

What time is it when T. rex comes to school?

Time to RUN!

Why did the elephants get kicked off the beach?

They wouldn't keep their trunks up.

How many video games can you
fit in an empty backpack?

One, after that it is not empty!

What is Yoda's brother's name?

Broda.

English teachers
[ing-glish tee-chers] phrase.

All English teachers eat synonym rolls
for breakfast, have an Instagrammer
account, and think that double negatives
are a big no-no.

Yesterday I got an Xbox for my little brother.

Best trade ever!

Where do baby monsters go during the work week?

Day SCARE centers.

Student: "It hurts when I move my arm like this."

School Nurse: "Then don't move your arm like that.

107

Books From Tesse Adams.
More Ages Coming Soon!

Made in the USA
Las Vegas, NV
17 December 2023

83061126R00066